HIGH VOLTAGE HABIB

Abhijit Naskar is the twenty-first century Neuroscientist whose contributions in Cognitive and Behavioral Neuroscience have helped the world tackle the issues of systemic racism, prejudice, hate, extremism, discrimination and biases more effectively. As an untiring advocate of mental health and universal acceptance, he became a beloved best-selling author all over the world with his very first book "The Art of Neuroscience in Everything". With his pioneering ventures into the Neuropsychology of beliefs and biases, he has hugely contributed in the eradication of religious and cultural differences in our world, for which he is popularly hailed as the humanitarian scientist, who takes the human civilization in the path of sweet general harmony.

HIGH VOLTAGE
HABIB

Gospel of
Undoctrination

ABHIJIT NASKAR

Also by Abhijit Naskar

The Art of Neuroscience in Everything
Your Own Neuron: A Tour of Your Psychic Brain
The God Parasite: Revelation of Neuroscience
The Spirituality Engine
Love Sutra: The Neuroscientific Manual of Love
Homo: A Brief History of Consciousness
Neurosutra: The Abhijit Naskar Collection
Autobiography of God: Biopsy of A Cognitive Reality
Biopsy of Religions: Neuroanalysis towards Universal
Tolerance
Prescription: Treating India's Soul
What is Mind?
In Search of Divinity: Journey to The Kingdom of Conscience
Love, God & Neurons: Memoir of a scientist who found
himself by getting lost
The Islamophobic Civilization: Voyage of Acceptance
Neurons of Jesus: Mind of A Teacher, Spouse & Thinker
Neurons, Oxygen & Nanak
The Education Decree
Principia Humanitas
The Krishna Cancer
Rowdy Buddha: The First Sapiens
We Are All Black: A Treatise on Racism
The Bengal Tigress: A Treatise on Gender Equality
Either Civilized or Phobic: A Treatise on Homosexuality
Wise Mating: A Treatise on Monogamy
Illusion of Religion: A Treatise on Religious
Fundamentalism
The Film Testament
Human Making is Our Mission: A Treatise on Parenting
I Am The Thread: My Mission
7 Billion Gods: Humans Above All
Lord is My Sheep: Gospel of Human
Morality Absolute
A Push in Perception
Let The Poor Be Your God
Conscience over Nonsense
Saint of The Sapiens
Time to Save Medicine
Fabric of Humanity
Build Bridges not Walls: In the name of Americana
The Constitution of The United Peoples of Earth

Lives to Serve Before I Sleep
When Humans Unite: Making A World Without Borders
All For Acceptance
Monk Meets World
Mission Reality
Citizens of Peace: Beyond The Savagery of Sovereignty
Operation Justice: To Make A Society That Needs No Law
See No Gender
The Gospel of Technology
Every Generation Needs Caretakers: The Gospel of
Patriotism
Aşkanjali: The Sufi Sermon
Mad About Humans: World Maker's Almanac
Revolution Indomable
When Call The People: My World My Responsibility
No Foreigner Only Family
Hurricane Humans: Give me accountability, I'll give you
peace
Ain't Enough to Look Human
Servitude is Sanctitude
Time To End Democracy: The Meritocratic Manifesto
I Vicdansaadet Speaking: No Rest Till The World is Lifted
Boldly Comes Justice: Sentient not Silent
Good Scientist: When Science and Service Combine
Sleepless for Society
Neden Türk: The Gospel of Secularism
Martyr Meets World: To Solve The Hard Problem of
Inhumanity
The Shape of A Human: Our America Their America
When Veins Ignite: Either Integration or Degradation
Heart Force One: Need No Gun to Defend Society
Solo Standing on Guard: Life Before Law
Generation Corazon: Nationalism is Terrorism
Mucize Insan: When The World is Family
Hometown Human: To Live for Soil and Society
Girl Over God: The Novel (Abi Naskar Adventures Book 1)
Gente Mente Adelante: Prejudice Conquered is World
Conquered
Earthquakin' Egalitarian: I Die Everyday So Your Children
Can Live
Giants in Jeans: 100 Sonnets of United Earth
Vatican Virus: The Forbidden Fiction (Abi Naskar
Adventures Book 2)
Karadeniz Chronicle: The Novel (Abi Naskar Adventures

Book 3)
Şehit Sevda Society: Even in Death I Shall Live
Handcrafted Humanity: 100 Sonnets For A Blunderful
World
Mücadele Muhabbet: Gospel of An Unarmed Soldier
Making Britain Civilized: How to Gain Readmission to The
Human Race
Dervish Advaitam: Gospel of Sacred Feminines and Holy
Fathers
Honor He Wrote: 100 Sonnets For Humans Not Vegetables
The Gentalist: There's No Social Work, Only Family Work
Either Reformist or Terrorist: If You Are Terror I Am Your
Grandfather
Woman Over World: The Novel (Abi Naskar Adventures
Book 4)

To all lovers of humankind.

In a world that peddles love sensible,
be love impossible.

CONTENTS

1. When Peace Demands A Bulldozer

A shortsighted world teaches you that there is either violence or nonviolence. But guess what! Real life is beyond the grasp of a world that can only think in terms of binary. Real life situations are rarely ever straightforward enough to be defined in terms of binary or duality.

Hence, a confused world remains confused till kingdom come, without the slightest desire for growth. Because as far as this prehistoric world is concerned, there can be no reality outside a binary reality.

Reality is a rainbow with infinite colors. Only when you realize this, can you start taking baby steps beyond biases. Let me elaborate.

I am no Gandhi, that I would rather let people be tortured by imperialist morons than raise my hand in their defense. I am no Guevara either, that I would accept the loss of innocent lives in my fight for freedom. I am a whole, accountable, thinking human being living in a world still infested with and run by cruelty and biases. Where the situation demands silence, I'll keep quiet, but if and where it demands a bulldozer, believe you me, no gun, no grenade, my bare hands will cause a riot.

The fact of the matter is, weak-willed creatures living in glass castles with their knee-deep advocacy of nonviolence won't last five minutes amidst the cruelties of the real world. And yet that's where life lies - in the streets and on the soil.

In this real domain of sweat and blood, there is no place for phony intellectual argumentation - all that works here is conviction. All that can survive here is either a character of substance or a character of cruelty.

This is no world for rich kids and their selfies - this is no world for phony materialistic snobs who waste more food than they eat. For this is the real world - the world that lives, the world that lasts - in sickness and in health - in uplift and in degradation.

2. Human Bulldozer (The Sonnet)

Human Bulldozer
(The Sonnet)

I am no Gandhi, that I'd sit quietly and spin a wheel,
While people suffer in the clutches of imperialism.
I am no Guevara either, that I would shoot anyone,
Who looks suspicious, in my revolution for freedom.
Gandhi and Guevara are two extremes of human struggle,
One glorifies submission, another heralds new oppression.
Neither is fit for an infant world aiming to be civilized,
For one lacks backbone, the other weaponizes assumption.
We may take a little from Gandhi, a little from Guevara,
Without rigidity we may administer them accordingly.
I am an accountable human living in a world run by biases,
So most times I'll keep quiet and act as a harmless dummy.
But whenever inhumanity goes overboard wreaking havoc,
The human bulldozer will rise to cleanse every epoch.

3. If You Wanna Know Life

If you wanna know life, if you wanna know joy, if you wanna know sorrow, then come down from your pedestal of luxury, from your castle of comfort - come down to the streets and onto the soil - and you won't just see people, you'll see the march of real humankind, you'll witness the dawn of real liberty - you'll realize how far a person would go to acquire just the fundamentals of life and living, not for themselves mark you, but for their family.

This realization, my friend, can't be taught through books, it can't be taught through bogus half-baked ideologies of the dead. To realize it, you gotta live it, you gotta live it like there is no tomorrow - you gotta live it like your life depends on it - because guess what! It actually does - to all those people on the streets, to all those whom you look down on as pedestrians, to all those who don't know a word of philosophy, and yet each of them is a living vessel of humankind's collective wisdom gathered through centuries of struggle.

Because struggle builds character, struggle makes you wise, struggle endows you with the real insight of life. And no ideology in the world is human enough and alive enough to teach you the worth of struggle, except struggle itself.

Too many ideologies, too little common sense - too much philosophy, too little friendliness - too many beliefs, too little conviction.

This won't do. If we want to breathe mettle into the world, this won't do.

If we want to straighten the backbone of society, this won't do.

Struggle is needed, unvarnished, unadorned, unaided struggle - not struggle for comfort, luxury and relaxation, but for community, life and rejuvenation.

Only with such struggle I stand in front of you today as the character I am. Every true giant of history who has anything to do with the uplift of humankind, is born of such struggle. No struggle no civilization.

4. No Struggle No Life
(The Sonnet)

No Struggle No Life
(The Sonnet)

Ain't no life without struggle,
Ain't no heart without heartbreak.
Ain't no destination without the journey,
Ain't no courage without some dread.
Ain't no clarity without some confusion,
Ain't no serenity without suffering.
Ain't no contentment without disappointment,
Ain't no resilience without failing.
Ain't no mindfulness without mindlessness,
Ain't no uplift without some devastation.
Ain't no knowledge without ignorance,
Ain't no salvation without self-annihilation.
Ain't no I without the Us, without the We.
Ain't no We, unless the norm is nonbinary.

5. No Struggle No Life

The day the struggle ends so does the civilization. This is why luxury is the last place for the development of civilization. There can be no growth in the lap of luxury, either for the individual or for the society.

Luxury is the antithesis of life. Vanity is the antithesis of life. Self-aggrandizing is the antithesis of life.

Simpler the life, more substantial the life.

Simpler the character, more substantial the character.

Simpler the civilization, more substantial the civilization.

And you know what makes a person simple on the outside and substantial on the inside?

Struggle.

This requires stepping across ideologies, or to be more accurate - it requires stepping across ideological loyalty - across ideological allegiance.

You want to pledge allegiance?

Pledge allegiance to humanity, not to some bookish ideology of some dead ancestors.

And what is this allegiance business in the first place!

What you love you protect, whom you love, you protect - there's no allegiance here, there's no loyalty - it's just love - it's just life - unideological, undoctrinated, unphilosophized life.

And that's what's needed - unideological, undoctrinated, unphilosophized life, and a lot of it. Don't let no book and no backboneless baboon chain you to their cold, apathetic definition of world and worldliness.

6.   Diversity is No Gimmick
(The Sonnet)

Diversity is No Gimmick
(The Sonnet)

Diversity is no gimmick,
Diversity is no belief.
Diversity is life itself,
Diversity is uplift.
Diversity is sanity,
Diversity is joy.
Diversity is monsoon,
After a drought most dry.
There ain't no humanity,
If there is no diversity.
We ain't no human,
If inside we have no amity.
It ain't enough to talk of toleration!
Each of us is to be the vessel of unification.

7.   Either World or Worldliness

When coldness is the norm, worldliness is beastliness. But the moment the warm, gentle, bold and accountable being wakes up in each human, worldliness of the world will slowly but surely start to turn into loveliness.

Loveliness comes from you, beastliness comes from you - whatever happens to this world it's because of you - it's because of us. Like it or not, this is life - like it or not, this is the law that dictates the destiny of society, it dictates the destiny of an entire species.

As a matter of fact, there is no such thing as destiny, it's just a bunch of headstrong individuals hell-bent for a purpose - so much so, that they'd rather stop breathing than stop realizing their purpose.

Purpose defines a person.

What is your purpose?

Not your social status, not your educational qualifications, not your bank balance, not your faith, not your nationality - what is your purpose - as a living breathing human being?

And mark you, I am not talkin' about a self-serving purpose. As always, I am talkin' about a world-serving purpose - a purpose that doesn't just lift you but the world as well. In fact, your uplift lies in the uplift of the world. Your uplift lies in the uplift of your neighborhood, your uplift lies in the uplift of your society.

8.   The Human Way

Uplift of the individual lies in the uplift of the collective. And here's the interesting bit. When U takes preference over I, indoctrination becomes undoctrination.

Many are obsessed with the notion of second coming of one of my humanitarian predecessors. But let me tell you a secret, which is actually no secret at all, at least to those with some common sense.

There is no messiah, only mind taking care of mind.

There is no savior, only soul taking care of soul.

There is no peygamber (messenger), only people taking care of people.

Sharing not sneering, caring not scaring - that is the human way.

There is no place for scoffing, there is no place for coldness. If our ultimate goal was to build a world of concrete and cold, why the hell did we have to leave the caves in the first place? At least there was no hypocrisy in the life of a caveman.

Animal life is beautiful for there you find truthfulness, but there is nothing more disgusting than an animal pretending to lead a human life. The animal that pretends to be human is no human, but the animal who acknowledges and tames their innate animality is the first human.

Human is known by behavior, not by appearance. Human is known by kindness, not clothes.

I'll say it to you plainly.

Hay sólo una cultura para mí - amabilidad. Hay sólo una religión para mí - amor. Hay sólo una nacionalidad para mí - humanidad.

For me there is only one culture – kindness. For me there is only one religion – love. For me there is only one nationality – humanity.

9. Beyond Traditions

Humanidad - humanity - that is our prime identity, that is our prime purpose, that is our existential core - not intelligence, not appearance, not fame and fortune. People worry about artificial intelligence, for they don't understand it. As a behaviorist, I worry about human intelligence, for the potential of artificial intelligence is nothing compared to that of human intelligence.

Therefore I say, Artificial Intelligence is not the problem – heartless, senseless, reckless human intelligence is. If we spent half as much intelligence on lifting society as we do on insecurities and self-obsession we'd have cleansed this world of all its major troubles in a matter of months.

It's okay to have insecurities, what's not okay is to be run by insecurities. Yet that's exactly how life is run - that's exactly how the world is run. This won't do - if we want things to change, this won't do. This absolute olympian allegiance to one's insecurities won't do.

And let me tell you this. Once you free yourself from the clutches of your own insecurities, no tradition in the world will be able to keep your innate humanity from blooming beyond bounds.

Bloom my friend, bloom beyond bounds!

Gone are the days of medieval notions like messiah, savior, second coming and all that nonsense. It is time for everyday, ordinary human action.

You asked me what my mission is.

I'll tell you in simple words.

I wanna see each of you turn into a messiah of your own part of the world.

Each individual is to become the peace maker and peace keeper of their own communities, no matter who they are, what they are, or where they are.

10. Nonsense of Truth

In my thirty years of existence I've come to the realization that all talk of truth is nonsense. Because even though we assume truth to be absolute and universal, in reality, in our human world no one truth is universal or absolute, it's all relative. The only force absolute and universal is love - there's nothing higher, braver or wiser.

Take wars for example. Each side would say, they are fighting for truth. But how can it be? If both parties are fighting for truth, why is there war in the first place? That's because in all these circumstances either both sides are fighting primed by lies or one side is aggressing and the other is defending.

This has nothing to do with truth and all that. Rather it only is a revolting reminder of the fact that we as a species are still stuck in a stoneage past, so much so that any tribal moron could just invade the borders of another country with the same old cockeyed, prehistoric tendency of conquest as that of the savages in the jungle.

But in the midst of all this tribal chaos, I'd like to point out one simple fact.

Putin and Russia are not the same thing. Russia is represented by the people of Russia, whereas Putin represents Putin.

Extraordinary crisis requires extraordinary restraint. So, be cautious that your hate for Putin doesn't spill over onto the Russian people.

When Putin has become a spoilt brat, it's up to the Russian people to be the responsible adult and give him a good spanking. And believe you me, although there are some Russians who are still supporting Putin's atrocities in the name of patriotism, a great portion of the Russian civil society is standing up to that moron like the rest of the world.

11. War is Expensive
(The Sonnet)

War is Expensive
(The Sonnet)

War is expensive, peace is free,
Yet war is petty, peace is priceless.
War is childish, peace is for adults,
Yet war is complex, peace is child's play.
War is for fools, peace is for the sage,
Yet sages sustain war, deeming peace foolish.
War is strain on the brain, peace only needs love,
Yet intellectuals justify war, calling peace rubbish.
War is good for maintaining control over the people,
Hence imperialists peddle war in the name of justice.
But all imperialists are the fault of the civilians,
All wars are a failure of our civilized citizenship.
No war is tougher than the civilians of the world.
Exercise that potential to abolish all imperial gall.

12. To Heal or To Hate

Don't be like the nitwit Americans of January 6 who felt threatened by the equalization of the American people, instead, be like those brave Russians who have the guts to stand up for life, liberty and equality of their neighbors, even at the risk of being persecuted as traitor to their country.

Often times, state and nation turn out to be two completely different agencies, even though theoretically they are supposed to be one and the same. In these situations we must throw away all bookish notions of democracy and act out of plain, ordinary common sense humanity.

And in that common sense humanity we shall find healing.

You see, every crisis gives us two options - the option to hate, and the option to heal. The option we choose says a lot about our character. It takes character to love beyond bounds, to hate it takes none.

Besides, those who have realized love in every pore of their anatomy, love for life, love for people, love for the world - have no time for petty hate.

Heck, they don't even have any affinity to the things in which this materialistic society usually seeks happiness.

You know why?

Because, these lovers, these healers, have realized, the more you seek happiness in vacation, possession and admiration, the more miserable you'll be. Forgetting all that lift another soul, and you'll have all the happiness you truly need.

13. What is Happiness

What is Happiness? Happiness is a myth. It doesn't exist. What we call happiness is merely a temporary sensation of excitement that we receive upon the fulfillment of our expectations.

It's not happiness, it's addiction.

And since we have made a society out of this insane pursuit of addiction, our brain is never at a healthy state to actually fathom and more importantly produce true happiness.

And what is true happiness?

Contentment.

You've been working for hours. You haven't had the time to even have some water. Finally you finish your work and drink a glass of water. The sheer feeling of joy that you receive at that moment - that's happiness, that's contentment.

You haven't been near your loved ones for days, for you've been away for work. Finally you get home and take them in your arms - that's happiness, that's contentment.

Now let me tell you what is not happiness, what is in fact an unhealthy addiction which only ruins a person's life both mentally and physically.

You've been using the same smartphone for over a year now. Suddenly the brand announces the release of a new model. And you get all hyped up to buy that model, despite the fact that you don't really need it. That's addiction - that's an illness.

You visit a new place on vacation. But instead of experiencing that place with your heart, you bring your phone out and waste the entire vacation on taking pictures to post on social media.

That's addiction, that's illness. You know why? Because when you get home, you realize, you have plenty of pictures of the vacation on your phone alright, but you have no meaningful memory of that place in your heart.

In usual circumstances, our brain doesn't distinguish between addiction and true joy. It can only do that, when we stop running and start living. Because at the end of the day, joy is not about fulfilling expectations, joy is about learning to live beyond expectations.

14. Realization of Happiness

54

Now let me ask you once again - what is happiness? And where will you find it?

The happiness of a parent lies in the welfare of their children, the happiness of a reformer lies in the welfare of the people - particularly those people that this snobbish world takes for granted - particularly those people at the expense of whose happiness this maladjusted world enjoys its daily luxuries and conveniences.

That is why I say, there is no time for swag, there is no time for selfies - only thing needed is service - uncorrupted, uncompromising, unbent service - what's needed is selflessness.

But then again, those who are concerned with swag, what do they know about service!

Those who throw away more clothes, than they wear, what do they know about service! Those who waste more food than they eat, what do they know about hunger! Those who have had an abundance of everything in life, what do they know about the everyday struggle for the fundamentals of living - what do they know about the fight of life!

I have nothing to say to these possession-mad nincompoops. But to the humans I say, throw away your luxury, then come and talk to me - then come and hold my hand.

Luxury is the enemy – it is the enemy of the individual, it is the enemy of the collective, it is the enemy of humankind.

Renouncing all luxury, we have to get down to the dust and dirt of the soil and the street. Only then shall we be able to lift this society. Only then shall we be able to lift our home.

15. How Can Anybody Be Okay

Scholarly debate won't do - intellectual argumentation won't do - ideological intimidation won't do. What's needed is a heart of honey primed by the steel-strong conviction of collective uplift.

And I mean collective uplift - that is, the uplift of everybody -- not just the rich, white, christian, straight males - but everybody - the uplift of women, the uplift of the poor, the uplift of the colored, the uplift of the queer, the uplift of each and every person on earth, across the ignorance-induced divisions and discriminations of our prehistoric days.

Someone once rightly said, "women belong in all places where decisions are being made."

I say, F*** it! Women belong. Period.

Then just the other day, someone rather primitively said, don't say gay. I say, say gay anyway, for compliance to discrimination is the coward's way. And more importantly, compliance to discrimination is a silent endorsement of discrimination.

So, no matter what, in the face of discrimination, in the face of injustice, in the face of inhumanity, don't be silent. Whatever you do, don't be silent.

Answer me this.

How can anybody be okay, when some pompous, puffed-up, maladjusted, addlepated, blowhards keep impeding efforts of equality and assimilation, as if it's not 2022 AD, but 2022 BC!

I tell you, I for one, am not okay.

But guess what!

No matter how loudly the hyenas howl, they can never overpower a lion's roar.

No matter how ghastly the animals behave, it cannot undermine a human's endeavors.

I won't say that you won't ever face defeat, but I can tell you this - no act of genuine humanity ever goes to waste. No life of a true human ever goes to waste, that is, when you choose to live as human on the inside, and not just on the outside.

16. Undoctrination Sonnet

Undoctrination Sonnet

63

If we teach kids history,
They say we're indoctrinating them.
If we immunize them against disease,
They say we're microchipping them.
If we teach kids science,
They say we're practicing blasphemy.
If we teach kids biology,
They say we're messing with their identity.
With such mentality of a caveman,
How on earth did you manage to conceive!
I guess, to raise a human takes common sense,
But to make a baby takes only genital breach.
Hence it is more reason for reason to persevere.
There is no way we can let stone age reappear.

64

17. The Chupacabra Sonnet

The Chupacabra Sonnet

Chihuahuas need guns for strength,
They feel naked without concealed carry.
To them I say, with all humility,
Open your eyes muchacho - ¡chupacabra aquí!
You may keep your gun, I won't say a word,
But don't confuse them to be your safe haven.
Own them in secret, but think of using them,
And you'll face the wrath of this kraken.
You may conceal, you may carry, if law allows,
But dare not raise your gun at a reformador.
To the wounded stranger I am ointment,
But to the inhuman vermin I am volcano.
Carrying a gun every moron feels like superman.
Stand up to cruelty unarmed, then you are human.

18. Civilization is Not A Place
(The Sonnet)

Civilization is Not A Place
(The Sonnet)

No matter who likes it not,
Say Gay anyway.
Compliance to discrimination,
Is the coward's way.
A true leader once said, women belong in,
All places where decisions are being made.
I say, fudge it all,
Women just belong, period.
They say, they don't want their kids,
To be hurt learning history.
I say, if learning history makes you hurt,
You are in dire need of therapy.
Civilization begins when we acknowledge our primitiveness.
Civilization is not a place, it's a people, it's a process.

19. The Empowered Sonnet

The Empowered Sonnet

75

Woman empowered is civilization empowered.
Dream empowered is progress empowered.
Parents empowered is children empowered.
Teachers empowered is future empowered.
Don't defund the police, use those funds,
To send the officers to behavioral therapy.
To have an understanding of justice and order,
We must have a grip over our impulses and biases.
Discrimination don't disappear if we shut our eyes,
Each of us must live as an antidote to discrimination.
Ignorance doesn't become knowledge when peddled by scripture,
Better burn all scriptures if they peddle hate and division.
To conquer our biases and stereotypes is to conquer inhumanity.
To expand our heart beyond assumption is to empower humanity.

20. Sonnet of Single Mother

Sonnet of Single Mother

There is no greater superpower,
In the world than a single mother.
Far superior to the world leaders,
Is the resolve of a single mother.
Wanna learn to build a society?
Wanna become a nation builder?
Spend a couple of months as pupil,
At the feet of a single mother.
Want there to be peace and progress?
Hand social reins to single mothers.
Stand by them as aide with commitment,
Lo and behold, the healing appears.
A mom empowered is a world empowered.
A single mom empowered is creation empowered.

21. Revolutionizing Revolution

I say, no more sitting quiet on the couch hoping for a magical intervention from a mystical and fictional heaven. Heaven is to be built out of our own sweat and blood.

Vamos muchachos! Tenemos un mundo para construir. Tenemos un mundo que ayudar. Tenemos un mundo para igualar. Tenemos un mundo que levantar.

Come, my friends! We have a world to build. We have a world to help. We have a world to equalize. We have a world to lift.

Para todos su familia es el mundo - para mí el mundo es mi familia. The world is my family - it is your family - it is the family of every single creature who dares to call themselves human. For this very sense of universal familyhood is what makes a human – it's what makes us one humanity.

Only such human has electricity flowing through their veins, rest have ice water. Only such human can act beyond the two extremes of Gandhi and Guevara and be original.

Revolution is a beautiful word, but at the same time, it is an ugly world. It is a beautiful word because it holds the possibility for a truly civilized and just world. But then again, it is an ugly word, because it is ridiculously easy for a revolutionary to turn into the new oppressor without even being aware of it.

Hence, it's not enough to be a revolutionary, you gotta be a conscious revolutionary - one who is well aware of their own biases and assumptions. You have no idea, how many innocents were shot to death at the command of Guevara! Because, though his intentions were noble, he started to see imperialists everywhere.

I admit that the circumstances were unusual, but the point I am making is that, the revolutionaries of today must not repeat the mistakes of the revolutionaries of yesterday. Being brave ain't enough, we must act wiser.

In short, we must first revolutionize the very idea of revolution. We must revolutionize revolution.

22. Enough Clowning

Civilization doesn't fall from the sky, it springs from the human heart. Justice doesn't grow on trees, it springs from the human heart. The heart giveth, the heart taketh away.

Be kind to the heart, and the heart will be kind to you. To see good in the world, we must first be the good in the world.

So, awake, arise o timelord, give this world your undaunted love and accountability. And in time the universe will fall at your feet, and time itself will deliver you immortality.

Immortality is child's play, but you gotta be mad for the welfare of this world like a child, without all the practical nonsense of self-preservation. Love like a child, lift like a child, in a world of selfish adults, be a selfless smile.

A helping hand with a gentle smile can change the course of human history. Helping is rising, hating is drowning. Learning is climbing, judging is clowning.

Enough clowning!

Enough frowning!

It's time for sweating, it's time for sacrificing.

But guess what! Sacrifice is no piece of pie for everybody. Only the human of heart can give all to lift others, to lift the society, to lift the world.

The measure of a human is sacrifice, the pleasure of a human is sacrifice, the treasure of a human is sacrifice. That's what makes us a human, that's what makes us a lover, that's what makes us a nutter.

Lover also, nutter also - that's the motto.

There is no love without a nutter - that is no nutter without love. Those who live this law, they alone live, rest only keep seeking life in products and puritanism, and end up dead without even tasting a drop of life - human life that is.

23. Service Over Selfies Sonnet

Service Over Selfies Sonnet

Awake, Arise O Timelords,
Oh makers and breakers of destiny!
Give this world accountability,
And time will give you immortality.
I don't want your shallow folllows,
I do not want your fancy likes.
Reach out as friend to someone in need,
That'll be my life's greatest prize.
Social media stats are no sign of character,
Fan following is no measure of a being.
Service over selfies, that is the motto,
Helping over hogging, that is living.
Life begins with the end of self-obsession,
Life self-obsessed is nothing but excretion.

24. Superpower of The Oligarch

People make life, not products. The sooner you realize this, the sooner you'll reclaim the natural wellbeing of your mind and body. Comfort, luxury, conveniences - all these have made slime out of living beings, which has not only ruined human health, but more importantly it continues to sustain a paradigm of greed and disparity.

In short, your everyday, so-called harmless materialistic obsession is the root of all disparities and divisions in the world - economic, cultural, religious and whatever.

Let me put it into perspective. Forget sacrifice for the time being. Your desire for unrestrained comfort is the oligarch's superpower. Cut yourself off from luxury, and you'll cut off the oligarchs from their powers. Cure for oligarchy is not policy reform, but lifestyle reform - from a materialistic one to a simple, non-luxurious one.

Wealth tax or not, the filthy rich will always find a way to stash their dough away from the eyes of the government, that is, away from the eyes of the people. So, if you want oligarchs to fall, you are the one who has to rise first, as an everyday, ordinary citizen - as a sane, civilized, self-regulated human being - such a being to whom service, sacrifice, altruism are not mere theoretical concepts, but the way of everyday life.

That's how a society is built. That's how a civilization is built. That's how humankind advances - not through technological advancement, but through psychological advancement - the advancement of the everyday, ordinary, individual human psyche - by the advancement of the psyche of the citizen.

Civilization is built one citizen at a time - not one government at a time.

And who is that citizen?

Who else!

25. Be A Tesla (The Sonnet)

Be A Tesla
(The Sonnet)

In a world full of Elon Musks,
Be a Dan Price.
Use entrepreneurship to instill equity,
Not as a vessel of disparity's vice.
In a world full of Jordan Petersons,
Be a Jiddu Krishnamurti.
Use intellect to expand perception,
Not to turn back the clock of primitivity.
In a world full of Donald Trumps,
Be a Dolly Parton, be an Ocasio-Cortez.
Use fame and politics to alleviate anguish,
Not to feed on people's distress.
Let others adore the crook Edison all they wanna.
You for one be a Marie Curie, be a Nikola Tesla.

26. The Real CEO

You are to build yourself, if you are to build a civilization. This is the only way. You know why? Because you and the civilization are one and the same. Your sanity is the civilization's sanity, your accountability is the civilization's accountability, your electricity is the civilization's electricity.

You know why there is so much power outage in the world? Because the humans are unaware of their own electricity, both metaphorically and literally. And one who realizes their inner electricity and brings it out to electrify the whole world, is the true CEO of the world.

I don't care for being the CEO of some puny anti-humanitarian company, for I am already a CEO - I am the CEO of planet earth - I am the Chief Evolution Officer of the human world - so is every single human whose responsibility towards society outweighs their primeval drive for narcissism and self-preservation.

In every age, in every time, there'll come ten of us Chief Evolution Officers to make mincemeat of the megalomaniacal ploy of anti-humanitarian giants while driving human evolution in a humane direction.

Human evolution is no longer dependent on even mother nature's whim, then how can we let our evolution be determined by a bunch of ostentatious oligarchs.

Hear me well - human evolution is human design – it is the design of human beings, not savage fiends. If savages were to dictate the evolution of humankind, then why on earth did we have to leave the jungle and the caves in the first place!

27. High Voltage Sonnet

High Voltage Sonnet

Once upon a time I said to thee, Awake, Arise,
Stop not till thou write thy destiny!
Two score later I said to thee,
Give me blood, and I'll give thee liberty!
Time passed and some life got much fancier but,
Division and disparity remain ever so horrid.
We have made great strides on the outside yet,
In the mental domain we remain ever so brutish.
A twenty watt brain once accountable,
Electrifies the universe.
But when selfish and indifferent,
Even 20 million of them cannot do diddly-squat.
Fetch those cables from your spinal cord,
Awake, arise, and electrify this dampened world!

28. Leave The Jungle

It's not enough to leave the jungle, we have to throw the jungle off our heart. It's not enough to leave the caves, we have to smash the caves within. Only then shall we instill the greenery of gentleness in this cold world of concrete.

Concrete is cold, yes - but it doesn't have to be.

Does it!

You have to decide, then you have to dictate - you have to dictate the direction of your neighborhood, you have to dictate the direction of your society, you have to dictate the direction of this world.

Because you know what happens when a human doesn't dictate their own destiny! Some fancy moron walks in like they own you, and dictates your life, in a way that is most beneficial for not you, or the society, or the world, but for themselves.

I won't sugarcoat it.

When the humans don't dictate the terms, the savages do. Yes it is a battle, it is a war - and this war will continue so long as humankind exists - and more importantly, this war will persist so long as there is the slightest desire in the human heart for ascension - so long as there is the slightest desire in us for the attainment of civilization.

You see, civilization is a myth - it doesn't exist, at least not the way we are taught it does. Civilization is not a static state - you know what it is - civilization is our everyday, ordinary, and very much dynamic drive for reform.

Civilization is a process, not a place.

And more importantly it is an endless process.

Reform is civilization, stagnation is degradation. Expansion is elevation, exclusion is extinction. Inclusion is illumination, discrimination is delusion.

29. No Time For Motivation

Discard all delusion, and serve the world like your life depends on it, for it does. Real humans don't boast. Their sense of service says it all about their character.

Mark you, these are not to be confused with those shallow, narcissistic sissies who need motivation to accomplish every little task in their life. In a world of shallowness and narcissism motivation is yet another commodity that can be gift-wrapped and sold to all those suckers who are just begging to be ripped off.

But here's the thing. I am no motivation salesman. I am not here to ease your life, I am here to make an absolute mess of your life. I am here to turn it upside down. I am here to turn you into a dynamite of pure humanitarian potential.

I have no desire whatsoever to ease the so-called pains of luxury. I am here to turn each and every one of you into a living painkiller to the actual anguish of the human world.

Every human is a painkiller, every human is a revolution. To argue over philosophy you need intellect, to lift a soul you need none. And remember this, suckers seek motivation, reformers seek self-annihilation.

Reformers don't have time for motivation, for they are too accountable. It's only the lazy bums who chase after motivation, and thus end up as the new commodity themselves for an entire new profession of motivation-salesman.

Mark you, I am not saying reformers don't feel gloomy at times, they don't feel broken at times - on the contrary, these are the most broken people on earth, but unlike the materialistic morons of the world, reformers don't have time to sit and whine about their gloom. Reformers embrace their gloom and turn it into strength instead of ending up the slave.

30. In Your Trust (The Sonnet)

In Your Trust
(The Sonnet)

My soldiers don't smoke and drink,
Though they may try them for experience.
They don't look at another sexually,
Without their wholehearted consent.
I made myself the human,
I want to see in the world.
Touch my work only after,
You've renounced being self-absorbed.
I didn't annihilate my entire life,
So that you may turn me into another cult.
Never you use me to boost your ego,
Or as an excuse for intellectual outburst.
Do not be Naskar, be the Naskar 2.0.
I leave my homeworld in trust of yours.

31. High Voltage Human

My beings with volcanic veins don't have time for motivation - my soldiers of sacrificial spirit don't have time for serenity - for each of my soldiers is a bulldozer incarnate - they have only one goal, one purpose, one mission in mind - the absolute abolition of inhumanity from the face of the earth.

Whining is one thing, reform is another. Whining is for sissies, reform is for heroes. As a matter of fact, every reformer is a hero, and every hero is reform incarnate.

Reform and reformer are not two, but one.

The reformer doesn't bring reform, the reformer is the reform. I am the reform, you are the reform, each and every responsible human on earth is a living reform. For reform is life, reform is sentience, reform is expansion.

Anything that lives, anything that is sentient, anything that expands, is the very spirit of reform, it is the very seed of reform.

Reform is just another name for responsibility. Where there is responsibility, there is reform. Where there is indifference, there is fall.

If you must fall, don't fall with indifference, fall in love - fall in love with your neighborhood, fall in love with your society, fall in love with the entire world. And from that very love all reform will come alright.

No judgment, no mockery, no grudge, no assumption - just fall. Fall head over heels for the world, like you did for your first love. Remember the loss of appetite, remember the sleeplessness, remember the constant desire to see them - once you feel that kind of intense attachment to the world, that day the world will have a true lover - that day the society will have a high voltage habib (beloved) – a high voltage human.

32. True Genius

In all this time, I have realized one simple fact - true genius is the one of the heart, not of intellect. Because intellect-less heart, though exploited a lot, still does good, whereas heartless intellect, with or without the awareness of it, ends up only exploiting others.

But here's the thing, even true genius of intellect is not without its fair sense of responsibility towards the society. It's only the genius of half-baked intellect that has absolutely no sense of service towards society - the only sense they have towards society, is that of domination or control.

That is why one of the guardians of nuclear physics, Albert Einstein though initially encouraged the US government in a letter, to develop a nuclear weapon of our own against the Nazi nuclear program, ended up being an outspoken activist of nuclear-disarmament, and called his letter to Roosevelt "one great mistake of life".

That is why the mother of radioactivity, Marie Curie never made a dime out of her discovery of radium, because to her, even amidst obscurity, science was service, unlike most so-called scientists of the modern world.

That is why the man who literally electrified the world with his invention of alternating current, Nikola Tesla embraced happily other people stealing his inventions, and died a poor man in his apartment.

You see, it's easy to make billions out of other people's pioneering work, the sign of true genius is an uncorrupted sense of service.

A homeless guy lifts a bread out of hunger, it's called burglary, but a cool-looking guy rips off an entire population, while spreading disparities wider than ever, it's called entrepreneurship.

What a world!

What a pathetic world!

If that's what you call entrepreneurship, then the jungles of planet earth are filled with entrepreneurs. You see, not all con-artists are billionaires, but every billionaire is a con-artist.

I have nothing to say to these con-artists, but I do pity those morons who make demigods out of these pathetic halfwits. If greed makes one genius, I better count my blessings that I am nothing but a dummy.

33. Be A Dummy

Be a dummy my friend - be a dummy! And if you want to learn about life, learn from the janitor, learn from the bartender, learn from the hooker, learn from the underpaid teacher, but don't make the materialistic mistake of glorifying billionaires and celebrities.

If you really want to have a just, equal and humane society, then first and foremost, eliminate your fetish for billionaires, socialites and royalty. We are the reason these moronic constructs have existed so far, and we are the ravager who are to wipe them off the face of earth.

I do not mean we are to kill these people, rather what I am talking about takes far more courage and character than it takes to do away with someone. What I am talking about is killing off the euphoria that hypnotizes the people whenever they hear the word billionaire or celebrity or royalty.

Behavior and behavior alone makes one worthy of glory, not status. You must move beyond status if you are to live as a sentient and civilized human being. Division of any kind, condescension on any basis, is poison on the fabric of a civilized society.

Equality begins in the mind. If in our own mind we have a pedestal for the billionaire and royalty, and no place for the janitor and the bartender, then even a thousand policy reforms won't be able to equalize such a cockeyed, internally broken society.

Fetish for status is violation of human dignity - it is a violation of the universal sanctity of human life. Therefore I say - no more fetish - no more euphoria - no more slavery of any kind - time has come for the human to rise as human - as hurricane human to inhumanity, and servant human to the discriminated and subjugated.

If I've told you once, I've told you a thousand times - only sultan is the servant - only law is the lover - only future is the reformer.

BIBLIOGRAPHY

Archer M., (2000), Being Human: The Problem of Agency. Cambridge University Press.

Adolphs R (2003) Cognitive neuroscience of human social behaviour. Nature Rev Neurosci 4: 165–178.

Adolphs R, Tranel D, Damasio AR (2003) Dissociable neural systems for recognizing emotions. Brain Cogn 52: 61–69.

Andresen, Jensine, and Robert Forman, eds. Cognitive Models and Spiritual Maps. Bowling Green, Ohio: Imprint Academic, 2000.

Azari, Nina, Janpeter Nickel, Gilbert Wunderlich, Michael Niedeggen, Harald Hefter, Lutz Tellmann, Hans Herzog, Petra Stoerig, Dieter Birnbacher, and Rudiger Seitz. "Neural Correlates of Religious Experience."

European Journal of Neuroscience 13, no. 8 (2001)

Agar, N. (2004). Liberal eugenics: In defence of human enhancement. London: Blackwell Publishing.

Alteheld, N., Roessler, G., Vobig, M., & Walter, R. (2004). The retina implant new approach to a visual prosthesis. Biomedizinische Technik, 49(4), 99–103.

Antal, A., Nitsche, M. A., Kincses, T. Z., Kruse, W., Hoffmann, K. P., & Paulus, W. (2004a). Facilitation of visuo-motor learning by transcranial direct current stimulation of the motor and extrastriate visual areas in humans. European Journal of Neuroscience, 19(10), 2888–2892.

Bernstein R.J., (1971), Praxis and Action: Contemporary Philosophies of Human Activity. Philadelphia: University of Pennsylvania Press.

Bernstein R.J., (1976), The Restructuring Social and Political Thought.

Bernstein R.J., (1983), Beyond Relativism and Objectivism: Science, Hermeneutics, and Praxis. Philadelphia: University of Pennsylvania Press.

Bernstein R.J., (1986), Philosophical Profiles. Philadelphia: University of Pennsylvania Press.

Bernstein R.J., (1991), New Constellation. Cambridge: MIT Press.

Birkhead, T. R., Johnson, S. D. & Nettleship, D. N. (1985). Extra-pair matings and mate guarding in the common murre Uria aalge. - Anim. Behav. 33, p. 608-619.

Beauregard, Mario, and Vincent Paquette. "Neural Correlates of a Mystical Experience in Carmelite Nuns." Neuroscience Letters 405, no. 3 (2006)

Benson, Herbert. Timeless Healing: The Power and Biology of Belief. New York: Scribner, 1996

Bose, Subhas Chandra. An Indian Pilgrim: An Unfinished Autobiography, Oxford University Press, 1997

Bogen, J.E.(1995a), 'On the neurophysiology of consciousness: Part I. An overview', Consciousness and Cognition, 4.

Bogen, J.E. (1995b), 'On the neurophysiology of consciousness: Part II. Constraining the semantic problem', Consciousness and Cognition, 4.

Bremner, J. D., R. Soufer, et al. (2001). "Gender differences in cognitive and neural correlates of remembrance of emotional words." Psychopharmacol Bull 35 (3).

Brothers, L. (2002). The social brain: A project for integrating primate behavior and neurophysiology in a new domain. In J. T. Cacioppo et al. (Eds.), Foundations in neuroscience. Cambridge, MA: MIT Press.

Buss, D. D. (2003). Evolutionary Psychology: The New Science of Mind, 2nd ed. New York: Allyn & Bacon.

Buss, D. M. (1989). "Conflict between the sexes: Strategic interference and the evocation of anger and upset." J Pers Soc Psychol 56 (5).

Buss, D. M. (1995). "Psychological sex differences. Origins through sexual selection." Am Psychol 50 (3).

Buss, D. M., and D. P. Schmitt (1993). "Sexual strategies theory: An evolutionary perspective on human mating." Psychol Rev 100 (2).

Blakemore SJ, Decety J (2001) From the perception of action to the understanding of intention. Nature Rev Neurosci 2: 561.

Colapietro V., (1988), "Human Agency: The Habits of Our Being." Southern Journal of Philosophy, XXVI, 2, pp. 153-68.

Colapietro V., (1992), "Purpose, Power, and Agency." The Monist, 75, 4 (October) pp. 423-44.

Colapietro V., (2004a), "C. S. Peirce's Reclamation of Teleology." Nature in American Philosophy, ed. Jean De Groot (Washington, D.C.: Catholic University Press of America), pp. 88-108.

Carey DP, Perrett DI, Oram MW (1997) Recognizing, understanding and reproducing actions. In: Jeannerod M, Grafman J (eds) Handbook of neuropsychology. Vol. 11: Action and cognition. Elsevier, Amsterdam.

Carr L, Iacoboni M, Dubeau MC, Mazziotta JC, Lenzi GL (2003) Neural mechanisms of empathy in humans: a relay from neural systems for imitation to limbic areas. Proc Natl Acad Sci USA 100: 5497–5502.

Chomsky Noam, (2017) Requiem for the American Dream

Chomsky Noam, (2016) Who Rules the World?

Chomsky Noam, (2010) How the World Works

Churchland, P.S. (1986), Neurophilosophy (Cambridge, MA: The MIT Press).

Churchland, P.S. & Ramachandran, V.S. (1993), 'Filling in: Why Dennett is wrong', in Dennett and His Critics: Demystifying Mind, ed. B. Dahlbom (Oxford: Blackwell Scientific Press).

Churchland, P.S., Ramachandran, V.S. & Sejnowski, T.J. (1994), 'A critique of pure vision', in Large- scale Neuronal Theories of the Brain, ed. C. Koch & J.L. Davis (Cambridge, MA: The MIT Press).

Coyle EF. Integration of the physiological factors determining endurance performance ability. Exerc Sport Sci Rev. 1995;23:25–63.

Crick, F. (1994), The Astonishing Hypothesis: The Scientific Search for the Soul (New York: Simon and Schuster).

Crick, F. (1996), 'Visual perception: rivalry and consciousness', Nature, 379.

Crick, F. & Koch, C. (1992), 'The problem of consciousness', Scientific American, 267.

Damasio, A (2003a) Looking for Spinoza. Harcourt Inc. Damasio A (2003b) Feeling of emotion and the self. Ann NY Acad Sci 1001: 253–261.

d'Aquili, Eugene. "Senses of Reality in Science and Religion." Zygon 17, no 4 (1982)

d'Aquili, Eugene. "The Biopsychological Determinants of Religious Ritual Behavior." Zygon 10, no. 1 (1975)

d'Aquili, Eugene. "The Myth-Ritual Complex: A Biogenetic Structural Analysis." Zygon 18, no. 3 (1983)

d'Aquili, Eugene, and Andrew Newberg. The Mystical Mind: Probing the Biology of Religious Experience. Minneapolis: Fortress Press, 1999.

Daly DD. 1958. Ictal affect. Am J Psychiatry.

Damasio, A. (1994) Descartes' Error: Emotion, Reason and the Human Brain. New York, Putnams.

Damasio, A. (1999) The Feeling of What Happens: Body, Emotion and the Making of Consciousness. London, Heinemann.

Darwin, C. (1859) On the Origin of Species by Means of Natural Selection. London, Murray.

Darwin, C. (1871) The Descent of Man and Selection in Relation to Sex. London, John Murray.

Darwin, C. (1872) The Expression of the Emotions in Man and Animals. London, John Murray; also published 1965, Chicago, University of Chicago Press.

Dawkins, M.S. (1987) Minding and mattering. In C. Blakemore and S. Greenfield (eds) Mindwaves. Oxford, Blackwell, 151-60.

Dawkins, R. (1976) The Selfish Gene. Oxford, Oxford University Press; a new edition, with additional material, was published in 1989.

Di Pellegrino G, Fadiga L, Fogassi L, Gallese V, Rizzolatti G (1992) Understanding motor events: A neurophysiological study. Exp Brain Res 91: 176–80.

Deikman, A.J. (2000) A functional approach to mysticism. Journal of Consciousness Studies 7(11-12), 75-91.

Delmonte, M.M. (1987) Personality and meditation. In M. West (ed.) The Psychology of Meditation. Oxford, Clarendon Press, 118-32.

Dennett, D.C. (1988) Quining qualia. In A.J. Marcel and E. Bisiach (eds) Consciousness in Contemporary Science. Oxford, Oxford University Press, 42-77.

Dennett, D.C. (1991) Consciousness Explained. Boston, MA, and London, Little, Brown and Co.

Dennett, D.C. (1995a) Darwin's Dangerous Idea. London, Penguin.

Dennett, D.C. (1998b) Brainchildren: Essays on Designing Minds. Cambridge, MA, MIT Press.

Dewhurst, Kenneth, and A. W. Beard. "Sudden Religious Conversions in Temporal Lobe Epilepsy." British Journal of Psychiatry 117 (1970)

Dewhurst K, Beard AW. Sudden religious conversions in temporal lobe epilepsy. 1970 Epilepsy Behav 2003

Devinsky O, Lai G. Spirituality and religion in epilepsy. Epilepsy Behav 2008.

Devinsky, O., Morrell, MJ, Vogt, BA. (1995) 'Contribution of anterior cingulate cortex to behavior', Brain, 118.

E. Horvitz, "One Hundred Year Study on Artificial Intelligence: Reflections and Framing," ed: Stanford University, 2014.

Eckhart Meister, Selected Writings

Egidi R., ed. (1999), "Von Wright and 'Dante's Dream': Stages in a Philosophical Pilgrim's Progress", in

In Search of a New Humanism: the Philosophy of G.H. von Wright, ed. by R. Egidi, Kluwer, Dordrecht.

Fadiga L, Fogassi L, Pavesi G, Rizzolatti G (1995) Motor facilitation during action observation: a magnetic stimulation study. J Neurophysiol 73: 2608–2611.

Fogassi L, Gallese V, Fadiga L, Rizzolatti G (1998) Neurons responding to the sight of goal directed hand/arm actions in the parietal area PF (7b) of the macaque monkey. Soc Neurosci Abs 24:257.5.

Frith U, Frith CD (2003) Development and neurophysiology of mentalizing. Philos Trans R Soc Lond B Biol Sci 358: 459.

Farah, M.J. (1989), 'The neural basis of mental imagery', Trends in Neurosciences, 10.

Finlay BL, Darlington RB (1995) Linked regularities in the development and evolution of mammalian brains. Science 268.

Freud, S. "The Interpretation of Dreams", 1900

Freud, S. "Selected papers on hysteria and other psychoneuroses" Journal of Nervous and Mental Disease 1909.

Freud, S. "The Origin and Development of Psychoanalysis", 1910

Freud, S. "Psychopathology of everyday life", 1914

Freud, S. "Beyond the Pleasure Principle", 1920

Frith, C.D. & Dolan, R.J. (1997), 'Abnormal beliefs: Delusions and memory', Paper presented at the May, 1997, Harvard Conference on Memory and Belief.

Gay, Volney, ed. Neuroscience and Religion. Plymouth, UK: Lexington Books, 2009.

Gazzaniga, M. S. (1985). The social brain. New York: Basic Books.

Gazzaniga, M.S. (1993), 'Brain mechanisms and conscious experience', Ciba Foundation Symposium, 174.

Geschwind N. "Behavioural changes in temporal lobe epilepsy". Psychol Med. 1979.

Gellhorn, E., Kiely, W.F. "Mystical states of consciousness: neurophysiological and clinical aspects." J Nerv Ment Dis. 1972;154:399-405.

Gilbert SL, Dobyns WB, Lahn BT (2005) Genetic links between brain development and brain evolution. Nat Rev Genet 6.

Gray JA. The Psychology of Fear and Stress. 2nd ed. New York, NY: Cambridge University Press; 1988.

Gloor, P. (1992), 'Amygdala and temporal lobe epilepsy', in The Amygdala: Neurobiological Aspects of Emotion, Memory and Mental Dysfunction, ed J.P. Aggleton (New York: Wiley-Liss).

Greenspan, S. I. and S. G. Shanker (2004). The first idea: How symbols, language, and intelligence evolved from our early primate ancestors to modern humans. Cambridge, MA: Da Capo Press.

Grady, D. (1993), 'The vision thing: Mainly in the brain', Discover, June.

Gallagher HL, Frith CD (2003) Functional imaging of 'theory of mind'. Trends Cogn Sci 7: 77.

Gallese V, Fogassi L, Fadiga L, Rizzolatti G (2002) Action representation and the inferior parietal lobule. In: Prinz W, Hommel B (eds) Attention & Performance XIX. Common mechanisms in perception and action. Oxford University Press, Oxford.

Gallese V, Keysers C, Rizzolatti G (2004) A unifying view of the basis of social cognition. Trends Cogn Sci 8: 396–403.

Goldman AI, Sripada CS (2004) Simulationist models of face-based emotion recognition. Cognition 94: 193–213.

Grèzes J, Costes N, Decety J (1998) Top-down effect of strategy on the perception of human biological motion: a PET investigation. Cogn Neuropsychol 15: 553–582.

Grèzes J, Armony JL, Rowe J, Passingham RE (2003) Activations related to "mirror" and "canonical" neurones in the human brain: an fMRI study. Neuroimage 18: 928–937.

Gross CG, Rocha-Miranda CE, Bender DB (1972) Visual properties of neurons in the inferotemporal cortex of the macaque. J Neurophysiol 35: 96–111.

Guevara Che, The Motorcycle Diaries, 1992

Hari R, Forss N, Avikainen S, Kirveskari S, Salenius S, Rizzolatti G (1998) Activation of human primary motor cortex during action observation: a neuromagnetic study. Proc. Natl Acad Sci USA 95: 15061–15065.

Hardy, G. H. (1940). Ramanujan. Cambridge: Cambridge University Press.

Hall, Daniel, Keith Meador, and Harold Koenig. "Measuring Religiousness in Health Research: Review and Critique." Journal of Religion and Health 47, no. 2 (2008)

Harris, Sam, Jonas Kaplan, Ashley Curiel, Susan Bookheimer, Marco Iacoboni, and Mark Cohen. "The Neural Correlates of Religious and

Nonreligious Belief." PLoS One 4, no. 10 (October 1, 2009)

Halgren, E. (1992), 'Emotional neurophysiology of the amygdala within the context of human cognition', in The Amygdala: Neurobiological Aspects of Emotion, Memory and Mental Dysfunction, ed J.P. Aggleton (New York: Wiley-Liss).

Halligan PW, Fink GR, Marshal JC, Vallar G. 2003. Spatial cognition: evidence from visual neglect. Trends Cogn Sci.

Handbook of Emotions, Edited by Michael Lewis, Jeannette M. Haviland-Jones, and Lisa Feldman Barrett, The Guilford Press; 3rd edition (2010).

Hameroff, S.R. and Penrose, R. (1996) Conscious events as orchestrated space-time selections. Journal of Consciousness Studies 3(1), 36-53; also reprinted in J. Shear (ed.) (1997) Explaining Consciousness-The Hard

Problem. Cambridge, MA, MIT Press, 177-95.

Harding, D.E. (1961) On Having no Head: Zen and the Re-Discovery of the Obvious. London, Buddhist Society.

Hardy, A. (1979) The Spiritual Nature of Man: A Study of Contemporary Religious Experience. Oxford, Clarendon Press.

Harre, R. and Gillett, G. (1994) The Discursive Mind. Thousand Oaks, CA, Sage.

Haugeland, J. (ed.) (1997) Mind Design II: Philosophy, Psychology, Artificial Intelligence. Cambridge, MA, MIT Press.

Hauser, M.D. (2000) Wild Minds: What Animals Really Think. New York, Henry Holt and Co.; London, Penguin.

Hebb, D.O. (1949) The Organization of Behavior. New York, Wiley.

Helmholtz, H.L.F. von (1856-67) Treatise on Physiological Optics.

Hess, EH (1975) "The role of pupil size in communication," Scientific American, 233(5), 110–12.

Heyes, C.M. (1998) Theory of mind in nonhuman primates. Behavioral and Brain Sciences 21, 101-48; with commentaries.

Heyes, C.M. and Galef, B.G. (eds) (1996) Social Learning in Animals: The Roots of Culture. San Diego, CA, Academic Press.

Hilgard, E.R. (1986) Divided Consciousness: Multiple Controls in Human Thought and Action. New York, Wiley.

Hilton, E.N., Lundberg, T.R. Transgender Women in the Female Category of Sport: Perspectives on Testosterone Suppression and Performance Advantage. Sports Med 51, 199–214 (2021).

Hitler, Adolf. Mein Kampf, 1925

Hodgson, R. (1891) A case of double consciousness. Proceedings of the Society for Psychical Research 7, 221-58.

Hofstadter, D.R. and Dennett, D.C. (eds) (1981) The Mind's I: Fantasies and Reflections on Self and Soul. London, Penguin.

Holland, J. (ed.) (2001) Ecstasy: The Complete Guide: A Comprehensive Look at the Risks and Benefits of MDMA. Rochester, VT, Park Street Press.

Holmes, D.S. (1987) The influence of meditation versus rest on physiological arousal. In M. West (ed.) The Psychology of Meditation. Oxford, Clarendon Press, 81-103.

Holmstrom, David. 1992, Christian Science Monitor

Holt, J. (1999) Blindsight in debates about qualia. Journal of Consciousness Studies 6(5), 54-71.

Holloway RL (1996) Evolution of the human brain. In: Lock A, Peters CR (eds) Handbook of human symbolic evolution. Oxford University Press, Oxford

Iacoboni M, Woods RP, Brass M, Bekkering H, Mazziotta JC, Rizzolatti G (1999) Cortical mechanisms of human imitation. Science 286: 2526–2528.

Iacoboni M, Koski LM, Brass M, Bekkering H, Woods RP, Dubeau MC, Mazziotta JC, Rizzolatti G (2001) Reafferent copies of imitated actions in the right superior temporal cortex. Proc Natl Acad Sci USA 98: 13995–13999.

Jeannerod M (1988) The neural and behavioural organization of goal-directed movements. Clarendon Press, Oxford.

Johnson-Frey SH, Maloof FR, Newman-Norlund R, Farrer C, Inati S, Grafton ST (2003) Actions or hand-objects interactions? Human inferior frontal cortex and action observation. Neuron 39: 1053–1058.

Jackson, F. (1982) Epiphenomenal qualia. Philosophical Quarterly 32, 127-36.

James, W. (1890) The Principles of Psychology (2 volumes). London, Macmillan.

James, W. (1902) The Varieties of Religious Experience: A Study in Human Nature. New York and London, Longmans, Green and Co.

Jansen, K. (2001) Ketamine: Dreams and Realities. Sarasota, FL, Multidisciplinary Association for Psychedelic Studies.

Jay, M. (ed.) (1999) Artificial Paradises: A Drugs Reader. London, Penguin.

Jaynes, J. (1976) The Origin of Consciousness in the Breakdown of the Bicameral Mind. New York, Houghton Mifflin.

Johnson, M.K. and Raye, C.L. (1981) Reality monitoring. Psychological Review 88, 67-85.

Kadim I, Mahgoub O, Baqir S et al. (2015) Cultured meat from muscle stem cells: a review of challenges and prospects. J Integr Agr 14: 222–233

Kandel, E. R. In Search of Memory: The Emergence of a New Science of Mind, W. W. Norton & Company (2007).

Kandel E. R. Schwartz JH, Jessel TM. Principles of neural sciences. New York; McGraw Hill, 2000.

Kanwisher, N. (2001) Neural events and perceptual awareness. Cognition

79, 89-113; also reprinted inS. Dehaene (ed.) The Cognitive Neuroscience of Consciousness. Cambridge, MA, MIT Press, 89-113.

Karn, K. and Hayhoe, M. (2000) Memory representations guide targeting eye movements in a natural task. Visual Cognition 7, 673-703.

Kennedy, H., & Dehay, C. (1988). Functional implications of the anatomical organization of the callosal projections of visual areas V1 and V2 in the macaque monkey. Behav. Brain Res., 29, 225–236.

Kentridge, R.W. and Heywood, C.A. (1999) The status of blindsight. Journal of Consciousness Studies 6(5), 3-11.

Kihlstrom, J.F. (1996) Perception without awareness of what is perceived, learning without awareness of what is learned. In M. Velmans (ed.) The Science of Consciousness. London, Routledge, 23-46.

Kosslyn, S.M. (1980) Image and Mind. Cambridge, MA, Harvard University Press.

Kosslyn, S.M. (1988) Aspects of a cognitive neuroscience of mental imagery. Science 240, 1621-6.

Kinsbourne, M. (1995), 'The intralaminar thalamic nucleii', Consciousness and Cognition, 4.

Kjaer, Troels, Camilla Bertelsen, Paola Piccini, David Brooks, Jorgen Alving, and Hans Lou. "Increased Dopamine Tone during Meditation- Induced Change of Consciousness." Cognitive Brain Research 13, no. 2 (April 2002)

Kölmel HW. 1985. Complex visual hallucinations in the hemianopic field. J Neurol Neurosurg Psychiatry.

Koenig, Harold. "Research on Religion, Spirituality, and Mental Health: A Review." Canadian Journal of Psychiatry 54, no. 5 (May 2009)

Koenig, Harold, ed. Handbook of Religion and Mental Health. San Diego, CA: Academic Press, 1998

Kraepelin E. Psychiatry: A Textbook for Students and Physicians. New York, NY: Science History Publications; 1990.

Lauglin, Charles, John McManus, and Eugene d'Aquili. Brain, Symbol, and Experience. 2nd ed. New York: Columbia University Press, 1992

Lakoff, G. and M. Johnson (1999). Philosophy in the flesh. Basic Books: New York.

LeDoux, J. E. (1996). The emotional brain. New York: Simon & Schuster.

LeDoux, J.E. (1992), 'Emotion and the amygdala', in The Amygdala: Neurobiological Aspects of Emo- tion, Memory and Mental Dysfunction, ed J.P. Aggleton (New York: Wiley-Liss).

Levin, D.T. and Simons, D.J. (1997) Failure to detect changes to attended objects in motion pictures. Psychonomic Bulletin and Review 4, 501-6.

Levine,J. (1983) Materialism and qualia: the explanatory gap. Pacific Philosophical Quarterly 64, 354-61.

Levine,J. (2001) Purple Haze: The Puzzle of Consciousness. New York, Oxford University Press. Levine, S. (1979) A Gradual Awakening. New York, Doubleday.

Levinson, B.W. (1965) States of awareness during general anaesthesia. British Journal of Anaesthesia 37, 544-6.

Lewicki, P., Czyzewska, M. and Hoffman, H. (1987) Unconscious acquisition of complex procedural knowledge. Journal of Experimental Psychology: Learning, Memory and Cognition 13, 523-30.

Lewicki, P., Hill, T. and Bizot, E. (1988) Acquisition of procedural knowledge about a pattern of stimuli that cannot be articulated. Cognitive Psychology 20, 24-37.

Lewicki, P., Hill, T. and Czyzewska, M. (1992) Nonconscious acquisition of information. American Psychologist 47, 796-801.

Manthey S, Schubotz RI, von Cramon DY (2003). Premotor cortex in observing erroneous action: an fMRI study. Brain Res Cogn Brain Res 15: 296–307.

Mesulam MM, Mufson EJ (1982) Insula of the old world monkey. III: Efferent cortical output and comments on function. J Comp Neurol 212: 38–52.

Naskar, Abhijit. "Homo: A Brief History of Consciousness", 2015

Naskar, Abhijit. "What is Mind?", 2016

Naskar, Abhijit. "Love, God & Neurons: Memoir of A Scientist who found himself by getting lost", 2016

Naskar, Abhijit. "Principia Humanitas", 2017

Naskar, Abhijit. "We Are All Black: A Treatise on Racism", 2017

Naskar, Abhijit. "Either Civilized or Phobic: A Treatise on Homosexuality", 2017

Naskar, Abhijit. "The Bengal Tigress: A Treatise on Gender Equality", 2017

Naskar, Abhijit. "Morality Absolute", 2017

Naskar, Abhijit. "Build Bridges not Walls: In the name of Americana", 2018

Naskar, Abhijit. "Fabric of Humanity", 2018

Naskar, Abhijit. "Citizens of Peace: Beyond the Savagery of Sovereignty", 2019

Naskar, Abhijit. "The Constitution of The United Peoples of Earth", 2019

Naskar, Abhijit. "Neurons Giveth, Neurons Taketh Away | Abhijit Naskar | TEDxIIMRanchi", 2019 https://www.youtube.com/watch?v=BNX-Q0ySm80

Naskar, Abhijit. "Mission Reality", 2019

Naskar, Abhijit. "Operation Justice: To Make A Society That Needs No Law", 2019

Naskar, Abhijit. "Every Generation Needs Caretakers: The Gospel of Patriotism", 2020

Naskar, Abhijit. "Hurricane Humans: Give me accountability, I'll give you peace", 2020

Naskar, Abhijit. "Revolution Indomable", 2020

Naskar, Abhijit. "Servitude is Sanctitude", 2020

Naskar, Abhijit. "Good Scientist: When Science and Service Combine", 2020

Newberg, Andrew, and Jeremy Iversen. "The Neural Basis of the Complex Mental Task of Meditation: Neurotransmitter and Neurochemical Considerations." Medical Hypotheses 61, no. 2 (2003).

Newberg, Andrew. "How God Changes Your Brain: An Introduction to Jewish Neurotheology", CCAR Journal: The Reform Jewish Quarterly, Winter 2016.

Newberg, Andrew, and Stephanie Newberg. "A Neuropsychological Perspective on Spiritual Development." In Handbook of Spiritual Development in Childhood and Adolescence, edited by Eugene

Roehlkepartain, Pamela King, Linda Wagener, and Peter Benson. London: Sage Publications, Inc., 2005

Newberg, Andrew. "The Neurotheology Link An Intersection Between Spirituality and Health", Alternative and Complimentary Therapies, Vol 21 No 1, February 2015.

Newberg, Andrew, Nancy Wintering, Dharma Khalsa, Hannah Roggenkamp, and Mark Waldman. "Meditation Effects on Cognitive Function and Cerebral Blood Flow in Subjects with Memory Loss: A Preliminary Study." Journal of Alzheimer's Disease 20, no. 2 (2010)

Nash, M. (1995), 'Glimpses of the mind', Time.

Nesse RM. Proximate and evolutionary studies of anxiety, stress and depression: synergy at the interface. Neurosci Biobehav Rev. 1999;23:895-903.

Nicolelis, Miguel. (2011) "Beyond Boundaries: The New Neuroscience of Connecting Brains with Machines--- and How It Will Change Our Lives", Times Books

O'Hara, K. and Scutt, T. (1996) There is no hard problem of consciousness. Journal of Consciousness Studies 3(4), 290-302, reprinted in J. Shear (ed.) (1997) Explaining Consciousness. Cambridge, MA, MIT Press, 69-82.

O'Regan, J.K. (1992) Solving the "real" mysteries of visual perception: the world as an outside memory. Canadian Journal of Psychology 46, 461-88.

O'Regan, J.K. and Noe, A. (2001) A sensorimotor account of vision and visual consciousness. Behavioral and Brain Sciences 24(5), 883-917.

O'Regan, J.K., Rensink, R.A. and Clark,].]. (1999) Change-blindness as a result of "mudsplashes." Nature 398, 34.

Ornstein, R.E. (1977) The Psychology of Consciousness (2nd edn). New York, Harcourt.

Ornstein, R.E. (1986) The Psychology of Consciousness (3rd edn). New York, Pehguin.

Ornstein, R.E. (1992) The Evolution of Consciousness. New York, Touchstone.

Penfield W, Faulk ME (1955) The insula: further observations on its function. Brain 78: 445– 470.

Penrose, R. (1994), Shadows of the Mind (Oxford: Oxford University Press).

Penrose, R. (1989), The Emperor's New Mind: Concerning Computers, Minds and The Laws of Physics (Oxford: Oxford University Press).

Persinger, "'I would kill in God's name' role of sex, weekly church attendance, report of a religious experience and limbic lability" Perceptual and Motor Skills 1997.

Persinger "Experimental simulation of the God experience" Neurotheology 2003.

Persinger, Corradini, Clement, Keaney, et al "Neurotheology and its convergence with neuroquantology" NeuroQuantology 2010.

Persinger, Koren and St-Pierre "The electromagnetic induction of mystical and altered states within the laboratory" Journal of Consciousness Exploration and Research 2010.

Persinger "Case report: A prototypical spontaneous 'sensed presence' of a sentient being and concomitant electroencephalographic activity in the clinical laboratory" Neurocase 2008.

Persinger and Saroka "Potential production of Hughlings Jackson's "parasitic consciousness" by physiologically-patterned weak transcerebral magnetic fields: QEEG and source localization" Epilepsy & Behavior 28 (2013).

Persinger. "The neuropsychiatry of paranormal experiences". J Neuropsychiatry Clin Neurosci 2001.

Persinger. "Neuropsychological bases of god beliefs", New York: Praeger, 1987

Persinger. "Temporal lobe epileptic signs and correlative behaviors displayed by normal populations", Journal of General Psychology, 1986

Perry BD, Pollard R. Homeostasis, stress, trauma, and adaptation. A neurodevelopmental view of childhood trauma. Child Adolesc Psychiatr Clin N Am. 1998;7:33.

Paré, D. & Llinás, R. (1995), 'Conscious and preconscious processes as seen from the standpoint of sleep-waking cycle neurophysiology', Neuropsychologia, 33.

Phillips ML, Young AW, Senior C, Brammer M, Andrew C, Calder AJ, Bullmore ET, Perrett DI, Rowland D, Williams SC, Gray JA, David AS (1997) A specific neural substrate for perceiving facial expressions of disgust. Nature 389: 495–498.

Phillips ML, Young AW, Scott SK, Calder AJ, Andrew C, Giampietro V, Williams SC, Bullmore ET, Brammer M, Gray JA (1998) Neural responses to facial and vocal expressions of fear and disgust. Proc R Soc Lond B Biol Sci 265: 1809–1817.

Puce A, Perrett D (2003) Electrophysiological and brain imaging of biological motion. Philosoph Trans Royal Soc Lond, Series B, 358: 435–445.

Ramachandran VS. Behavioral and magnetoencephalographic correlates of plasticity in the adult human brain. Proc Natl Acad Sci USA 1993; 90: 10413–20.

Ramachandran VS. Phantom limbs, neglect syndromes, repressed memories, and Freudian psychology. Int Rev Neurobiol 1994; 37: 291–333.

Ramachandran VS. Plasticity and functional recovery in neurology. Clin Med 2005; 5: 368–73.

Ramachandran VS, Hirstein W. The perception of phantom limbs. The D. O. Hebb lecture. Brain 1998; 121: 1603–30.

Ramachandran VS, Rogers-Ramachandran D, Cobb S. Touching the phantom limb. Nature 1995; 377: 489–90.

Ramachandran VS, Rogers-Ramachandran D. Phantom limbs and

neural plasticity. Arch Neurol 2000; 57: 317–20.

Ramachandran VS, Rogers-Ramachandran D. It's all done with mirrors. Sci Am Mind 2007; 18: 16–9.

Ramachandran VS, Rogers-Ramachandran D. Sensations referred to a patient's phantom arm from another subjects intact arm: perceptual correlates of mirror neurons. Med Hypotheses 2008; 70: 1233–4.

Ramachandran VS, Rogers-Ramachandran D, Stewart M. Perceptual correlates of massive cortical reorganization. Science 1992; 258: 1159–60.

Rizzolatti G, Craighero L (2004) The mirror-neuron system. Annu Rev Neurosci 27: 169–192.

Rizzolatti G, Fogassi L, Gallese V (2001) Neurophysiological mechanisms underlying the understanding and imitation of action. Nature Rev Neurosci 2:661–670.

Rock I, Victor J. Vision and touch: an experimentally created conflict between the two senses. Science 1964; 143: 594–6.

Rose´n B, Lundborg G. Training with a mirror in rehabilitation of the hand. Scand J Plast Reconstr Surg Hand Surg 2005; 39: 104–8.

Roberts, TA; Smalley, J; Ahrendt, D (December 2020). "Effect of gender affirming hormones on athletic performance in transwomen and transmen: implications for sporting organisations and legislators". British Journal of Sports Medicine. 55 (11): 577–583

Royet JP, Plailly J, Delon-Martin C, Kareken DA, Segebarth C (2003) fMRI of emotional responses to odors: influence of hedonic valence and judgment, handedness, and gender. Neuroimage 20: 713–728.

Rozin R Haidt J and McCauley CR (2000) Disgust. In: Lewis M, Haviland-Jones JM (eds) Handbook of Emotion. 2nd Edition. Guilford Press, New York, pp 637–653.

Saxe R, Carey S, Kanwisher N (2004) Understanding other minds: linking developmental psychology and functional neuroimaging. Annu Rev Psychol 55: 87–124.

S. J. Russell and P. Norvig, Artificial intelligence: a modern approach (3rd edition): Prentice Hall, 2009.

Singer T, Seymour B, O'Doherty J, Kaube H, Dolan RJ, Frith CD (2004) Empathy for pain involves the affective but not the sensory components of pain. Science 303: 1157–1162.

Smith A (1759) The theory of moral sentiments (ed. 1976). Clarendon Press, Oxford.

Schilling, Vincent. 2017, indian country today

Stein, Stephen K. 2017, The Sea in World History: Exploration, Travel, and Trade

Simonsen R (2015) Eating for the future: veganism and the challenge of in vitro meat. In: Stapleton P, Byers A (Hg). Biopolitics and utopia. Palgrave Macmillan, New York (2015), S 167–190

Tesla N. "My Inventions", 1919

T. R. Society, "Machine learning: the power and promise of computers that learn by example," ed. The Royal Society, 2017.

Tomasello M, Call J (1997) Primate cognition. Oxford University Press, Oxford.

181

HIGH VOLTAGE HABIB

www.ingramcontent.com/pod-product-compliance
Lightning Source LLC
Chambersburg PA
CBHW051256250726

48656CB00004B/1322